AMAZING MILITARY FACTS

AMAZING U.S. NAVY FACTS

by Mandy R. Marx

CAPSTONE PRESS
a capstone imprint

Pebble Plus is published by Capstone Press,
1710 Roe Crest Drive, North Mankato, Minnesota 56003
www.mycapstone.com

Library of Congress Cataloging-in-Publication Data
Names: Marx, Mandy R., author.
Title: Amazing U.S. Navy facts / by Mandy R. Marx.
Other titles: Amazing United States Navy facts
Description: North Mankato, Minnesota : Capstone Press, 2017. | Series:
   Pebble plus. Amazing military facts | Includes bibliographical references
   and index. | Audience: Age 4-8. | Audience: Grades K-3.
Identifiers: LCCN 2016016905| ISBN 9781515709527 (library binding) |
ISBN 9781515709848 (pbk.) | ISBN 9781515711193 (ebook (pdf)
Subjects: LCSH: United States. Navy—Juvenile literature.
Classification: LCC VA58.4 .M39 2017 | DDC 359.00973—dc23
LC record available at https://lccn.loc.gov/2016016905

Editorial Credits
Kayla Rossow, designer; Jo Miller, media researcher; Kathy McColley, production specialist

Photo Credits
Corbis: Steve Kaufman, 9; Photo provided courtesy General Dynamics Electric Boat, 17;
Shutterstock: BMJ, 23, 24; U.S. Navy photo by MC1 Chad J. McNeeley, 1, MC1 Martin Wright, 19,
MC2 Alex King, cover, MC2 Kyle D. Gahlau, 13, MC2 Ryan J. Batchelder, 5, MC3 Jonathan
Sunderman, 21, MCSN Cole C. Pielop, 15, MCSN S.A. Thornbloom, 7, PH3 Yesenia Rosas, 11

Note to Parents and Teachers

The Amazing Military Facts set supports national curriculum standards for science related
to science, technology, and society. This book describes and illustrates amazing facts about
the United States Navy. The images support early readers in understanding the text. The
repetition of words and phrases helps early readers learn new words. This book also
introduces early readers to subject-specific vocabulary words, which are defined in the
Glossary section. Early readers may need assistance to read some words and to use the Table
of Contents, Glossary, Read More, Internet Sites, Critical Thinking Using the Common Core,
and Index sections of the book.

Printed and bound in the USA.
009655F16

Table of Contents

Amazing Sailor Facts

Navy sailors guard oceans and waterways around the world. They even fight pirates at sea.

Amazing
On-the-Job Facts

Navy recruits train at boot camp.

Their final test lasts 12 hours.

It takes place on an indoor ship.

Do you have your own room?

Many sailors don't.

On submarines 140 sailors

share a room. They sleep

on bunks stacked three-high.

Aircraft carriers hold 5,500 people.
Workers wear different colored shirts
to show their jobs. This helps
keep order on deck.

Navy SEALs are high-level sailors.

Each year 1,000 men start

SEAL training. Only 250 finish it.

Amazing Vehicle Facts

Aircraft carriers are the Navy's biggest ships. They are longer than three football fields. They can hold up to 90 aircraft.

Could you live underwater?
Submarines can stay
underwater for 80 days.

Amazing Weapons Facts

Ships shoot torpedoes at targets.

Torpedoes move through the water.

Each one weighs up to 3,500 pounds

(1,590 kilograms). That's as much

as a male giraffe.

Missiles hit targets above water. Missiles can soar 1,500 miles (2,414 kilometers). That's as long as the East Coast of the United States.

Glossary

aircraft carrier—a warship with a large flat deck where aircraft take off and land

boot camp—a camp for training Navy sailors that lasts 8 weeks

missile—an explosive weapon that is thrown or shot at a distant target

pirate—a person who steals from ships at sea

recruit—a soldier in training

SEALs—a special forces group in the Navy; SEALs stands for SEa, Air, and Land

submarine—a ship that can travel underwater

target—an object at which to aim or shoot

torpedo—an underwater missile used to blow up a target

Read More

Bolt Simons, Lisa M. *U.S. Navy SEAL Missions: A Timeline.* Special Ops Mission Timelines. North Mankato, Minn.: Capstone Press, 2016.

Murray, Julie. *Navy Seals.* U.S. Armed Forces. Minneapolis: Abdo Kids, a division of ABDO, 2015.

Internet Sites

FactHound offers a safe, fun way to find Internet sites related to this book. All of the sites on FactHound have been researched by our staff.

Here's all you do:

Visit *www.facthound.com*

Type in this code: 9781515709527

Check out projects, games and lots more at **www.capstonekids.com**

Critical Thinking
Using the Common Core

1. What helps keep order on an aircraft carrier's deck? (Key Ideas and Details)

2. Would you rather live on an aircraft carrier or a submarine? Why? (Integration of Knowledge and Ideas)

Index